Guardia
Selection, ~~...~~

Copyright © 2022 by An Peischel
All rights reserved, including the right to reproduce this or portions thereof in any form whatsoever.

For more information, contact
An Peischel at goatsunlimited@gmail.com

To order autographed copies online:
goatsunlimitedkikos.com

Book photos by An Peischel

Editing and design by TurnKey Communications
(Oklahoma City, Okla.)

This publication was sponsored by
author and animal activist Pat Becker-Wallis, whose advocacy and books can be found at **DogTalkTV.com**

Publishing and printing
by Total Publishing and Media (Tulsa, Okla.)

This edition printed in 2022.

ISBN 978-1-63302-226-3

Dedication

It is to Bruce Cockrane of Williams Lake, British Columbia, Canada, that I owe many thanks for the amazing Akbash guardians he provided Goats Unlimited.

Hortense Joaquin of Makawao, Maui, Hawaii, whose perseverance and dedication helped Goats Unlimited become successful; I am grateful.

Contents

Introduction 1
1 Breeding Stock Selection 4
2 Whelping, Feeding and Early Healthcare 12
3 Facilitating Successful Guardian Dogs 18
4 Training the Owner 28
  About the Author 33

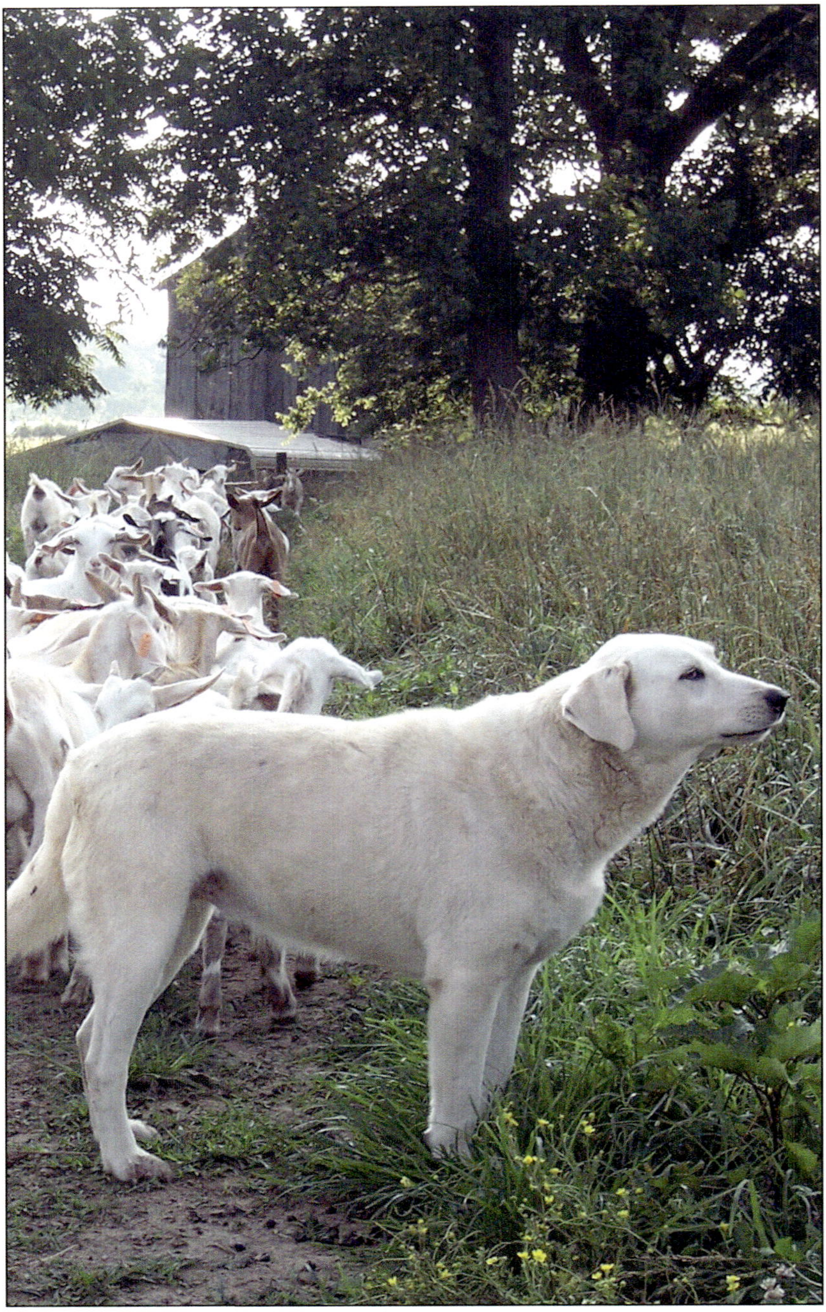

Introduction

BEFORE MOVING OUR Goats Unlimited business to north-central Tennessee, we operated in the Sierra Nevada range of northern California. The area had a significant population of mountain lions, bears and eagles—all potential threats to our goats.

Using five livestock guardian dogs, two Great Pyrenees and three Akbash, we began a land-cleaning project in a forested area of the Sierras with a dense understory and ladder fuel. An extended stay by our goats could consume much of this fuel and reduce the danger of wildfire.

We fenced an area with portable, three-strand electric polywire and introduced our guardian dogs to check for predators and become familiar with the terrain. Afterward, our goat mob entered the area and began browsing. The mob was checked daily.

Upon entering the fenced area one day, I was shocked to find one of the Pyrenees guardian dogs lying on top of a goat with blood all over both of them. Initially horrified at the thought of the dog attacking the goat, I realized on closer inspection that the dutiful guardian had suffered severe injuries while protecting the goat. The injured Pyrenees was bleeding heavily from gaping holes in his throat area and skin torn from his shoulder blades. He was also having trouble breathing.

The goat did not have a wound or scrape at all. I later surmised that a young male mountain lion had perpetrated this attack. I would never know the severity of the attacker's wounds, but they must have been serious enough to discourage his intentions to feast on any of our goats.

As I tried to pick up the injured dog, one of his hind legs dangled pathetically. Somehow, I managed to get him into my truck and to the veterinarian. After surgery and many months of recovery, he went back to work doing what he was meant to do.

This guardian dog had performed superbly at the critical moment when his services were needed most. Our canine protectors

Bred by ancient farmers in the Pyrenees Mountains between France and Spain, the Great Pyrenees has long protected flocks from predators like wolves and bears while showing a tolerance and affinity with the animals in its charge.

also gave us security against the bears and eagles in northern California.

Through my many years of experience with guardian dogs, I have come to admire and appreciate their devotion to protecting herd animals. While these dogs may fiercely protect their charges, they generally display gentleness, patience and tolerance to nonthreatening creatures around them. Their endearing qualities are many.

This book is intended to provide the reader with useful information to select, nurture and maintain this kind of guardian dog for the protection of livestock, especially goats.

1

Breeding Stock Selection

GOATS UNLIMITED is presently located in the rolling hardwood hills of the northern midsection of Tennessee. Our major predators are coyotes, bobcats, fox, hybrid wolves, buzzards, and domestic pack dogs. Recently, however, both a bear and mountain lion were caught on a nearby game camera.

The business setting for Goats Unlimited puts guardian dogs in both neighborhood locations and in densely vegetative areas with few people.

Breeding Stock Selection

We perform land cleaning and enhancement, and restoration of marginal lands, riparian areas, and stream banks. Our Kiko meat goats are also used to abate invasive weeds.

Our type of business puts our guardian dogs in situations where they could be patrolling in a neighborhood setting with people all around or in densely forested areas with humans rarely encountered. The region's extremes of weather, topography and vegetation test the livestock guardians' survival skills.

The dogs we breed are selected from ranches and farms that actively use these dogs as livestock guardians for both sheep and goats. Both the dam and sire of these dogs are required to work in physical conditions (terrain, predator-type, weather) as similar to ours as possible. The dogs must be physically sound by health examinations and structurally correct in hindquarters, forequarters, head, skull, and other physical characteristics,

Just like the predators that threaten herd animals, guardian dogs are nocturnal. It's important that their handlers remember this.

including chest, ribcage, back, feet, gait, tail, weight and size. They should be representative of their breed's standard.

We do not breed our guardians until they have proved successful as livestock guardians in their own right and have Orthopedic Foundation for Animals examinations (OFAs) confirming no evidence of hip dysplasia or osteochondritis (inflammation of bone or cartilage). They are also a minimum of two years old and display a gentle temperament toward humans.

For our breeding purposes, we also look for specific character traits that fit this region's environment, predation pressure, and management program. The Great Pyrenees and the Akbash are our favorites for guarding our goats. Always remember, these dogs are nocturnal—so are the predators.

The Great Pyrenees

The Great Pyrenees (commonly called Pyrenees Mountain Dog in Europe) is mentioned in documents hundreds of years

The Great Pyrenees shows minimal aggression toward humans—important as they could be patrolling in areas with people all around.

Breeding Stock Selection

The Great Pyrenees' thick coat protects it from winter rain, hail and snow but can readily collect burrs and thorns, as seen in the tail of the Pyrenees above.

old, owing its origin to the plateau of Tibet. It started as one of the Mastiff family and came to Europe with the Aryan hordes. Isolated for centuries in the Pyrenees Mountains between France and Spain, they guarded the flocks on the region's high, secluded mountain slopes.

They have a natural guarding instinct, protecting with their very lives those placed in their protection. Large and powerful, Pyrenees have great stamina and a coat for protection against both foe and adverse weather. They express an air of quiet confidence and tolerance, and are aristocratic.

Tolerant of people, the Pyrenees is well suited to neighborhood land-cleaning, restoration and weed-abatement projects, which can vary in size from twenty to 160 acres. These dogs show little aggression toward humans. Their thick coats protect them from the winter rain, hail and occasional snow in Tennessee. The dogs are expected to find their own shelter and protect themselves from the elements.

The Akbash

The Akbash originated in western Turkey centuries ago specifically for the guarding of sheep. Their main predators were wolves, wild dogs, jackals and bears. White in color, their shorter-length double coat is shed annually. Long-legged, muscular and strong, they have a fleet appearance and a build for speed and stamina. They have extraordinarily keen eyesight and hearing. They are ideal for forest, brush and rangeland operations.

Akbash are more aggressive to predators, possessing a strong maternal and guarding instinct and a forceful independent nature. Their speed and agility come from their sighthound ancestor, the Turkish greyhound, and their power from a Mastiff-type dog. They display a variety of body types.

Goats Unlimited's first Akbash breeding pair came from Bruce Cockrane in British Columbia, Canada. The female was power-

Bred by Turkish shepherds to protect their flocks, the Akbash have a fleet appearance and a build for speed and stamina.

Breeding Stock Selection

Akbash generally display a more aggressive attitude toward predators and possess a strong maternal and guarding instinct.

ful and stoutly built. The male was more athletic and agile.

The Akbash crossed with the Great Pyrenees reduces the dense coat of the Pyrenees. The coat of the crossbred is much shorter and has proven advantageous in hot, humid climates. The cross is exceptionally athletic like the Akbash, yet the personality and the bone structure of the Pyrenees is usually maintained. The crossbred guardians have the same black pigmentation around the eyes, nose and mouth as do the originating two breeds.

The Anatolian Shepherd and the Kangal

We are partial to the Pyrenees and Akbash guardian dogs at Goats Unlimited, but we also use the Anatolian Shepherd and Kangal with good results.

The Anatolian Shepherd originated in Anatolia (central Turkey) descending from powerful hunting dogs from Mesopotamia. Similar to the Akbash, they are rugged, large-bodied and strong with superior sight and hearing. The breed is agile, fast and extremely independent. They sport a thick double coat.

Guardian Dogs for Goats

Anatolian Shepherds have been used to guard livestock against wolves, bear, jackals and cheetahs.

The Anatolian Shepherd hails from central Turkey. A descendant of powerful hunting dogs, the breed is noted for its superior sight and hearing.

At left on facing page: An early Mastiff-type dog from Turkey, Kangals are recognizable by their black facemask.

Breeding Stock Selection

The Kangal originated in the Sivas Province of the central Anatolia region of Turkey and is of an early Mastiff-type dog. They are protective, loyal, gentle, courageous and very independent. When confronting a predator, their tactic is to intimidate the intruder (usually wolves), and when necessary use their agility and high speed to attack. Kangal's have a dense, thick undercoat for insulation in severe winters and an outer layer that repels snow and water. They are recognizable by their black facemask.

Kangals have a dense, thick undercoat for insulation in severe winters and an outer layer that repels snow and water. Above, a male Kangal babysits an Akbash pup.

2

Whelping, Feeding And Early Healthcare

ONCE THE SELECTED DOGS are bred, they receive extra nutrition (27 percent crude protein and 18 percent fat) with a daily vitamin and mineral supplement of readily absorbent

Growing fast, pups will be twice their birth weight by day five and need high levels of nutrients for the rapid growth of their long bones.

calcium and phosphorus. The bred females are used for guarding on close-in acreage to allow daily monitoring as whelping day approaches. Approximately a week before whelping, they receive booster parvovirus and seven-way vaccinations.

At Goats Unlimited, they are whelped out in the brush with the goats. It is left up to the dam to provide a "safe area" for her pups and to guard them. I check them from a distance with binoculars, leaving everything up to the dam. If the above scenario is not practical due to pending weather or pasture rotations, I whelp in an area with a stable flooring surface and fresh wheat straw. The dams will want to dig and nest, increasing the potential for suffocation or burial of a pup.

Our goat does often come by and eat some of the wheat straw. They like to hang out with the dam, and the pups readily get attached to the goats. Pups are born in litters of five to ten with an average birth weight between 1.5 and 2.5 pounds.

Before and after whelping, the dam receives added nutrition from a daily cooked meal of goat meat, a gravy bullion base with suet, supplemental vitamins and minerals,

At Goats Unlimited, it is left to the dam to provide a safe area for her pups and to guard them.

Eyes on these pups start opening at twelve to fourteen days old, at which time they are started on warm goat milk.

goat milk, and cooked brown rice. The new mom is given free choice to consume all she wants of both this mixture and a high-quality dry puppy food in a self-feeder.

Growing exceptionally fast, the pups will be twice their birth weight by day five. They need high levels of nutrients for the rapid growth of their long bones. Their eyes begin opening about twelve to fourteen days of age, and their eyes and nose start turning black. They are then started on warm goat milk.

A liquid mineral and vitamin supplement is added to the goat milk. The enriched milk is offered four times every twenty-four hours. The pups should be allowed to drink all they want.

I also put the dam's feed in a blender and serve it to the pups in a shallow baking pan for cookies. The pups can be placed right in the pan. They slime around and slurp up the mix. Mom will finish what they don't eat—and then she really enjoys cleaning up the pups!

At three weeks, the pups start eating a more solid cooked diet of mashed rice, dry puppy food soaked in goat milk, shredded and cooked goat meat, and a vitamin-mineral supplement. By the time they are five weeks old, they are chewing on dry puppy food but still receiving a meal of cooked meat daily.

At five weeks, they are chewing on dry puppy food and a daily meal of cooked meat. At six-weeks old, they are consuming a daily, evening meal of dry puppy food soaked in goat milk with cooked meat. Because these large breeds experience such rapid bone growth, it is vitally important to provide a balance of calcium, phosphorus and vitamin D3 until they are about eighteen months old. Between three and six months they may grow from thirty to 100 pounds.

Preventive Healthcare

At two days old, both the front (single) and rear (double) dewclaws are removed from the Great Pyrenees pups. All pups receive a five-way parvovirus vaccination at six and nine weeks, a seven-way vaccination (canine distemper, adenovirus type-2, coronavirus, parainfluenza, parvovirus and Leptospira bacterin) at twelve and fifteen weeks of age, and at twenty weeks another

After consuming his food from his baking-pan feeder, this enterprising pup turns his feeding pan into a bed.

parvovirus vaccination.

At about twelve weeks, a veterinarian should be consulted about the dogs' susceptibility to an area's tickborne diseases (Lyme disease, Rocky Mountain spotted fever, lone star, Asian tick disease, and ehrlichiosis). At sixteen weeks they are vaccinated against rabies.

At three months, they begin a lifelong monthly heartworm prevention program. Males are neutered at ten to twelve months, and females spayed about this same time. This timeframe is recommended by a veterinarian to minimize the susceptibility to cruciate ligament injuries. They are also microchipped at this time.

At one year, all the dogs begin an annual program for seven-way vaccination and rabies.

Litters of ten to twelve pups are not uncommon for breeds of guardian dogs, which can make for a challenge when trying to place individual pups with mature guardian dogs while the youngsters are undergoing facilitation.

Summer heat and humidity necessitates shearing the Great Pyrenees to prevent hotspots and matting, but never closer than two inches. They also need shearing if vegetation consists of blackberry vines, burdock and cocklebur. Their long coats can get tangled and full of burrs.

3
Facilitating Successful Guardian Dogs

I RECENTLY HAD AN INDIVIDUAL call to discuss the training of livestock guardian dogs. For a while I listened, but at the same time thinking to myself: *Train? I don't train. I facilitate success.* Everything I do—the selection of breeding

The intense natural instinct of guardian dogs to protect their charges should be allowed to self-express rather than instilled through training.

stock, whelping, exposure to different classes of goats and other livestock species, experience with varied terrain and different predators—is managed so that the maturing pups are given every chance to succeed on their own.

Every experience for a pup has to be positive. The pup needs to feel in control, and their intense natural instinct to guard needs to be self-expressed.

Bonding With the Livestock

Our dog breeding is timed so that the pups are born within the same timeframe as kidding (February through April and October through December). During any year several litters of guardian pups are born. When pups open their eyes, they see many "kid" eyes staring back at them, checking them out. The kids are cautious around the pups and are tolerant when the pups start waddling around interrupting the kids' nap time.

Kidding takes place in solar-powered electric fencing (four- to five-strand polywire or electro-netting) so the pups learn at a very early age where they are to stay. They have a great respect

With pups born in the same timeframe as the kids, they are better able to develop and bond. The kids are cautious around the pups but tolerant.

When her pups are six weeks old, the dam's supplemental meal is eliminated and she receives dry food only, thus initiating the process of drying off her milk. The weaning process has begun.

for the electric fence—it only takes one time of contact and their memory is imprinted forever.

The pups need to be *completely bonded* with the goats for them to be successful guardians. In their first few months, I do not pet the pups, nor do I let anyone else. They are handled only when receiving vaccinations or heartworm medication. At Goats Unlimited we run an old horse with the goat mob so the pups can get used to other species in their guardian regimen.

The pups will come around to "check in" when one goes into the pasture to check on the goats. The pups' presence around humans is acknowledged only with a quick pat on the head, and they are encouraged to "get back to the goats." Once they are completely bonded with their charges, then an extended head pat and neck rub—an affectionate acknowledgment to them—can be given.

The guardians are usually about three to four months old before they should receive this acknowledgment by humans. Each pup, however, is an individual maturing at a different rate than littermates, so take care that they are totally bonded with the livestock before befriending. And always remember, *the guardians are for the goats*.

Weaning the Pups

Once the pups are six weeks old, the supplemental meal for the dam is eliminated, and she reverts to dry food only. This initiates the process of "drying off" the dam's milk. The pups are encouraged to eat more food in individual pans, and the self-weaning has begun. By the time they are eight weeks old, they have weaned themselves.

We leave the dam with the pups if self-weaning has been successful. This allows the pups to travel with their mother and start to learn the ropes of a successful guardian. Should self-weaning not succeed, the dam is removed from the pasture, and an older, neutered male is placed with the pups as teacher-mentor. The pups stay with the kids until the kids are weaned at three and

If self-weaning is successful, a pup stays with its mother to learn to be a guardian. Should self-weaning not succeed, the pup may be placed with an older neutered male as teacher-mentor.

one-half months.

Once the kids are weaned, it's time to introduce the herding dogs (Border Collie, New Zealand Heading Dog and Huntaway). The guardian pups are still in the "apprehensive-curious" phase, so they more readily accept the herding dogs. As the goats are moved to different areas to clean, brush and browse, the pups are mustered with the goats by the herding dogs. The pups learn to travel with the mob and not to challenge the herding dogs.

The weaned goats are separated into two groups; the doelings (disbudded) and the wethers/bucklings (horned). At weaning, the pups and their teacher-mentor go with the doeling weanoffs. The pups will stay with the doelings until they are approximately the same height. It is important initially to keep the pups with a group of goats that are just slightly larger than the pups. This prevents the pups from trying to play with the goats. When they try to become too aggressive or assertive, the goats are large enough to dissuade the pups of this bad behavior.

Pups should initially be with a group of goats just slightly larger than the pups. This discourages the pups from trying to play with the goats.

As guardian pups mature, they are placed with a wethers/buckling mob or a dry doe mob, where a rambunctious pup is quickly taught good manners by these larger goats.

Once the pups reach a height where they need to be removed from the doeling mob, they are taken to the wethers/buckling group along with their teacher-mentor. It is also at this time they learn to eat from self-feeders.

Mentoring and Maturation

The wethers/buckling mob is physically larger and less tolerant of playful pups. They straighten out the rambunctious pups right away. It is at this point in "facilitating success" that the litter of pups is separated. Only pairs of pups are kept together with an older, mentor guardian.

When the two pups are almost as tall as the goats, they are moved to either a doe mob or a group of yearling bucks. These mobs are each being guarded by a minimum of three experienced dogs. The trainee guardians will stay with this size of goat until they are a year old, but they will be exchanged every few weeks so that all the pups will be with other mature guardians and other pups. The same two pups should not remain together.

I prefer to have only one pup with other guardians, but sometimes our litters of ten to twelve pups make this difficult. I like my dogs to be able to work together with any dog they may be placed with in the future. This is especially true when the main predator will be the wolf pack. The dogs need to adapt to and accept other livestock guardians and all classes of goats.

Introducing the Guardian to the Goats

At this point, these year-old pups can be sold and sent to their new homes. I ask the new owner if they have had a guardian dog with their goats. Are their goats used to a guardian dog, or is this a mob that has never had a guardian? It is critical that the pups are introduced to the goats correctly, or successful facilitation will not be achieved.

If the mob has had a guardian dog and is used to them in

If herding animals have never had a guardian dog, the introduction should be gradual to avoid stress on all parties.

Newly introduced guardians initially need to be kept in an enclosed area to learn the location of their new home.

their environs, then introducing a new guardian is less stressful. Should the goats never have had a guardian, they need to be introduced to the guardian slowly to avoid a stressful situation. This can be done by building a small corral divided into an area for the dogs and another for the goats. If things are peaceful after a few days, the dogs can be put with the mob.

The dogs need to be kept in a small, enclosed area to learn where their home is. When being fed, the dogs should be spaced apart to avoid fighting. I feed the dogs in the morning so they are more ready to protect during the time predators are active. For goats that insist on eating dog food, build a small enclosure that the goats cannot enter.

Evaluating the Maturing Dog

By the time they are one year old, the maturing dogs at Goats Unlimited have been in an area frequented by coyotes, bobcats, buzzards, fox, hybrid wolves and predatory domestic pack dogs.

Those not taken to a new home will continue training in this setting as yearlings. Between one and two years of age the guardians will participate in at least three kiddings.

At this time they should be observed for their active guardianship of the young kids and does, and their personalities and temperaments should be critically assessed. This is a major turning point. Any guardian not "passing the test" should be culled.

At about two years of age, they will go into densely forested areas and face the possibility of encountering bear, mountain lions and wolves. Here they are guarding in higher elevation vegetation with lots of dense brush, blackberries, downed timber, harvested areas, and trees. Guarding in the mountains will round out their guarding experiences. The goats they are guarding under these vegetative conditions are mature wethers and mature does. I now consider them mature, experienced livestock guardians.

At this point, the seasoned guardian dogs should do well at a new home in a different setting. The big day comes when the dogs are sent miles away to guard the goats or other livestock by themselves. They are on their own.

It takes time and effort to facilitate the success of a livestock guardian dog. They will save you many dollars and heartaches. A mature, experienced guardian is irreplaceable and commands respect. Goats Unlimited has been fortunate never to have lost a goat to predation with the use of guardian dogs, and we would not be successful without them. And it is to these livestock guardian dogs that I am grateful.

4

Training the Owner

I EARLIER STATED that I didn't really "train" guardian dogs, striving only to their success by staying out of the way of their natural instincts. With guardian dog owners, however, a little training is often needed. Some of this training is through on-the-job experience. I would like to share some of my experiences.

The Bear in the Tree

The forested areas of the Sierra Nevada mountains consist of national forests, privately owned timber companies, and private citizens. There are bear in the forests, and they have to be respected when utilizing a mob of mature wethers to reduce ladder fuel and minimize fire damage. As I was fencing-in a seventy-acre area to start browsing, I had several guardian dogs with me. I noticed that the three dogs were sitting at the base of a huge ponderosa pine tree. So, I looked up the tree as the dogs were and—a bear. The next plan was to get myself in my truck and my dogs in the trailer. When we returned to the area two days later, the bear had moved on.

Lesson: With guardian dogs, owner discretion is sometimes the better part of valor.

Training the Owner

It's a Team Effort (Part I)

Numerous rivers, creeks and small streams course through Tennessee. The major predators that travel these waterways are coyotes, bobcats, and *domestic pack dogs*.

Hiking along the Cumberland River after a late afternoon rain and a beautiful rainbow, I rounded a corner—and saw devastation. A pack of domestic dogs was shredding a mature wether. Where was the guardian? Unfortunately, there was only one. And he had the goat mob mustered together trying to guard them.

This is not the only incident with one guardian dog trying to protect his or her wards. A local farmer here in Tennessee lost twenty-three bred ewes from another attack by a pack of domestic dogs.

Lesson: You need to have a minimum of two guardians with a mob.

An attack on a goat by a pack of domestic dogs can prove just as devastating as an onslaught from a hungry mountain lion. A goat mob or group of any kind of herd animal needs a minimum of two guardian dogs for adequate protection. One of the guardians stays with its charges while the other(s) can directly intervene against the aggressor animal(s).

Guardian Dogs for Goats

Look Out from Above

Here in Tennessee, buzzards and black vultures pose a major problem at kidding, lambing and calving. They create major stress on the birthing mothers and will peck the eyes out of the newborn.

Guardians detect the buzzards and black vultures in flight and then react. They bark, chase and stay on guard—always keeping an eye on the sky. It can be important to have more than two guardian dogs on duty during a busy birthing time.

Lesson: An owner never knows where predator troubles lay, but a trusty guardian usually does.

It's a Team Effort (Part II)

Wild pigs are rampant in the Hawaiian Islands. It is very disheartening to be out in the pasture with the does at kidding time

Black vultures, buzzards and other birds of prey can pose a threat to newborns and put stress on new mothers. Guardians detect the black vultures and buzzards in flight and react before harm is inflicted.

Training the Owner

and come across a huge boar eating her new kids. This was my first experience with pigs and only one guardian dog on duty trying to protect the entire mob. Hence, a solution was a 30-30 Marlin and a neighbor who liked to hunt and process the meat.

Another option for minimizing the loss of kids and does from wild pig attacks is to utilize a different breed of dog. When confronted by wild pigs, the Akbash and Great Pyrenees act mainly as alert dogs and will remain with the mob while mustering the goats into a tight group.

As an extreme measure, Black Mouth Cur hounds or Catahoula Leopard hounds can be used with the lethal Dogo Argentino.

Wild pigs are a common threat to newborn herd animals in many parts of the United States. Typical guardian dogs like Akbash and Great Pyrenees act mainly as alert dogs for this threat, but more specialized dogs like Black Mouth Cur hounds, Catahoula Leopard hounds, and Dogo Argentino can help control wild pigs.

The hounds distract the pigs, then the Dogo Argentino goes in for the kill, crushing the pig's skull. The Dogo needs to be raised with the animals they protect and have to respond to the recall issued by the hunter. At all times the hunter has to be with the Dogo and be in control.

Using the Dogo Argentino, of course, is an extraordinary measure. But for an owner badgered by wild pigs, it can be an option.

<u>Lesson</u>: Different breeds of hunting dogs can be used to solve unique problems with predators.

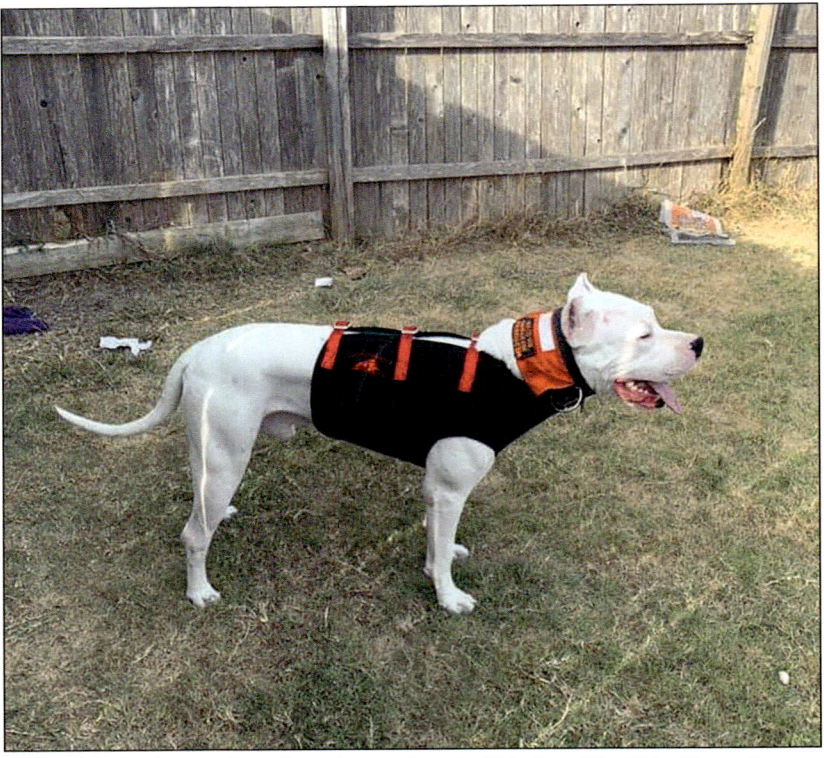

Dogs routinely used to directly confront wild pigs, like this Dogo Argentino above, can be fitted with lightweight body armor to protect their upper bodies.

About the Author

Born and raised on a livestock (beef, cattle, hogs) and crop (barley, hay, rye, buckwheat) farm, An Peischel lived in Uruguay on a sheep and beef cattle ranch. She received a MS degree in animal science from Universidad Federal de Santa Maria, Rio Grande do Sol, Brazil, and a PhD in range livestock nutrition from Kansas State University. She managed a beef cattle research center in Homer, Alaska, for the University of Alaska-Fairbanks, and taught at the University of Hawaii-Hilo and the University of California-Chico. She served as the goat and sheep extension specialist at Tennessee State University and the University of Tennessee. An has traveled extensively throughout South and Central America and Africa.

She started land enhancement with goats in 1985 and brought the first Kikos into the United States in 1990. Goats Unlimited is still in the land enhancement business thirty-six years later.